You Ain't Hungry Until I'm Starving

VID LAMONTE` BUGGS JR.

ISBN-13: 978-0692456293

ISBN-10: 0692456295

SAYING GRACE

Thank you God, the creator of all creations, for each and every blessing that has been, that is now and that will come.

2GBTG = To God Be the Glory

The secret is that there was never any secret at all. The truth lies within you and all around you. No idea is original and the truth cannot be destroyed.

MENU

NUTRITION FOR THE SOUL

Ever spent all day at school or work thinking about a piece of food that you've saved for yourself? Remember wanting that piece of food so badly that you didn't eat anything all day long? Finally you get home, go straight to the kitchen and guess what? Someone else has eaten what you are now starving for.

How about going to the store for some food? You ask everyone if they want something, everyone says no – but when you come back with your food, all of a sudden they all want it! Funny how nobody's hungry until you're starving.

These things happen even when food isn't involved. You can be starving for knowledge, attention, time, energy, etc., and it always seems like that's when someone else comes to you hungry for those exact same things. Just when you have your own issues to deal with, the rest of the world wants to dump their problems on you.

As living beings we're all in need of certain things to enable us to function and survive. We can crave understanding, love, success, happiness, and acceptance, among other things. We also desire things for pleasure, or to satisfy a need or feeling. Sometimes we want things simply because someone else has them.

It's ok to be hungry as long as you are not taking from someone who is starving - which is why this book is entitled *You Ain't Hungry Until I'm Starving.* I was tired of allowing people to suck up my own positive energy just when I needed it the most. In this book I offer what I believe is nourishment in different forms. You may not agree with everything that I say. However, the world and we as people are always changing, so with time and experience you may find that you can relate to the points that I've made here.

This book deals with many topics and covers every aspect of life. While reading, make an effort to disconnect yourself from the physical world and leave your preconceived thoughts behind. Here, you are neither male nor female, you have no race, and your age does not exist. You are oblivious to emotional demands and the quest for money. All I ask is that you proceed with an open mind, as well as an open heart, so that you may receive the nourishment that I have in store for you.

Bon Appetite! Enjoy.

1
COURSE ONE

Meal Preparation/Devotion

"With faith, discipline and selfless devotion to duty, there is nothing worthwhile that you cannot achieve." - Muhammed Ali Jinnah

2

THANKSGIVING

Mom and Dad; my blood sisters, Tanesha and Victoria; my best friends whom I think of as my brothers and sister, Zaki, Josh, Matt Lee, Jeff and Elyse - you all already know what it is, you were there when no one else cared to be, and you all have also kept it real with me.

My baby boy Dominique Mikail and my baby girl Sofia Lyn, I love you more than you will ever know.

Andrea, thank you for your love, patience and simply being you.

My cousin Dominique Pretlow, you were my right-hand man and I miss you every day, RIP.

Selena, Charisse, Tish and Heidi - thank you all for showing me what love really is between couples, and thank you for believing in me when I didn't believe in myself.

Marci Wise, thank you for editing and helping me bring my message and this book to life. Your support, advice and guidance is appreciated more than you will ever know. I am blessed to have worked on this project with you.

To all my professors and teachers - thank you for reaching me and allowing me to notice my potential.

To everyone that has come into my life, even for a blink of an eye; To all that serve as rebels against the system of wrongs; To those following their dreams no matter what others may say; To those who are spreading the True gospel of love; And to all of God's creations – I thank you for guiding, inspiring and influencing me.

Love you all; To God BE THE GLORY.

3
DEDICATION

Ms. Peggy McDonald Howells

I have decided to dedicate my book to all my family and close friends, however, I am specially dedicating this book to Ms. Peggy Howells. Peggy was a client that I personal trained back in 2007 - and she is so full of life. At the time, she was 72 years young, yet her spirit has always been so youthful and peaceful. Most importantly, her energy just uplifts people. She strives to accomplish many things, often telling herself when facing a difficult task, "I can do this." Although people may think she's crazy for doing the things that she does, she still goes after her goals. Case in point, she was in her forties when she went back to school to obtain multiple degrees - *after* having raised three children.

This lady is an inspiration to me. I love the way she pushes herself and gives everything she has to accomplish her goals. Just talking and listening to her has helped me to better discover who I am. We were two people from different worlds and times; she was 72 years of age, I was 27 – she, a white lady into opera and classical music - me, a black male who grew up in the hip hop culture - yet we were very connected, as if we grew up together.

There are three things that Peggy told me that have had a huge impact on my life. First, she said "There's no such thing as saying 'I'll try,' it's either you *will* do something or you *will not*." That's major, because we often lie to ourselves and others by saying "I'll try" when in reality if we really want something to happen, we'll make sure that it does. (As long as it's something that's truly within our control.)

The second thing she said was "I don't usually listen to rap music, but I like to hear it because the artists are relaying a message of what they see." Now, this was mind boggling to me because so often today it seems like the older generation does not try to understand the young – and instead just rejects most of the things that we're into.

Finally, I was intrigued when she told me that she thinks my friends and I are *very positive*. Of course, I feel the same way, however, this lady doesn't really know us, she just knows what I've told her - but this is special to me because she realizes that there are a whole lot of negative influences out here that we are striving to overcome. She sees the struggles of our generation and the struggles of others – which is pretty special.

Through Peggy, I've learned that you are never too old to live, dream, accomplish goals and believe. She also reminds me to never judge a book by its cover, because inside each book (person) there is something interesting, you just have to take the time to find it. Peggy serves as a great example of someone who is enjoying life (despite her age) - while some of us are so consumed with work, money, and problems that we forget to live. I suggest that we all find our own inner Peggy. The world can never have enough positive inspiration.

4

TO MY SON

Dominique Mikail, I named you after your cousin who passed away a few years ago. He was the closest person I had to being a brother. *Dominique* means "man of God" - while *Mikail* is derived from Michael, which means "faithful servant of God." It has been months since I last saw and held you, but that's alright because in due time, you will be back home with me. You are constantly on my mind - every second of every minute, of every hour of every day. It's a good thing that you will probably not remember what's happening at this moment. Just know that daddy loves you more than anything in this world. You make me proud to be a father; no matter what your mother is scheming and lying about in order to keep you away from me. She thinks that she is hurting me, which she is - but she does not understand how much she's hurting you.

I was so disappointed when she told her friend to tell me that she didn't want me in the delivery room, after she said for months that she wanted me there to witness your birth. But all that hurt was gone the moment I saw your little face and held you for the first time. My own little mini me. It's scary how much you look like me. Come to think of it, you have never cried in my arms - and I know you never will.

Although your mom is causing all this pain, you must always respect her, for she brought you into this world. It can be so hard to forgive and love a person after they've caused you pain – but no matter what, I forgive her. We all make mistakes and we all get a little crazy at times. And yes, I still love your mother with all my heart, but the love I have for her is not the love that couples share. You see, in loving you, I love her. We formed you together and to regret that would be to regret you – and I could never do that.

You've changed my life. Until you were born, I was simply content with my life but now I push myself every day to better things for you. So with this letter, this book, and my life, all is dedicated to you – my son.

5

JOHN LENNON

You were way ahead of your time, taken from us when we needed you most. However, your message and memory lives on. You told us to *Imagine* the world as one. You were not the only dreamer; you were not alone. In fact, I dream often - but the most peaceful was the *#9 Dream*.

Instant Karma has hit us over our heads but some of us still don't have a clue. Yet, we all shine on like the moon, the sun and the stars. You shined brighter than any star – a star that was so down to earth.

We know you never meant to make us cry. You were living on *Borrowed Time*. Since you've been gone, it's just *(Just Like) Starting Over*. Maybe we all should take your lead because like you said "Life is what happens while you're busy making other plans."

Every time I put my son to sleep I sing *Beautiful Boy*. Every man with a son can use this song to express the feeling their son gives them. John, we need your voice - and others like it - because we are at war. I, like many, wish we all could *Give Peace a Chance*. Maybe if the poor and the rich, the young and the old, the black, white, yellow and red can stop fighting, we truly can have a *Happy Xmas*. Is it going to take every kid to sing in unison, "war is over, if you want it, war is over now," in order for us to *Come Together* and *Give Peace a Chance?* I am a dreamer, but I know I'm not the only one. I wonder what would happen if we could actually make what we *Imagine* a reality.

6
COURSE TWO

Appetizers/Food for Thought

"How rich art is; if one can only remember what one has seen, one is never without food for thought or truly lonely, never alone." - Vincent van Gogh

7

WHO AM I

I am Created so perfect that I have imperfections.

I am the keeper of Earth, yet I destroy mother Earth on a daily basis.

I am the top of the food chain, yet in this food chain I am only a small piece of the pie.

I am both saint and sinner.

I am my best friend and yet my worst enemy.

I am an individual, yet I belong to so many groups.

I am the life of the party, yet I am a loner and an outcast.

I am not defined, but judged in the eyes of others by gender, race, sex, and sexual orientation.

I am an animal, however I look down on all other living creatures.

I am waiting for love, but I am the one that pushes love away.

I am wise and knowledgeable, however I know nothing.

Who am I? I ask You.

I'll tell you - I am You and You are Me.

8

HOW DO YOU KNOW ME?

You claim you know me.

I'm wondering how.

You say you have known me for years.

I ask, how can you know me

When I don't even know myself?

You say you know what I'm going through.

How can you?

When I don't even know what I'm going through.

You see, you can't possibly know - because you don't

understand.

That's like saying you know that 1+1=2 but you don't

understand how.

Still think you know me?

The more I grow,

The more I know

I know nothing at all.

And every time I change,

Everything remains the same.

You have yet to know yourself,

So, how do you know me?

9

REMEMBER MY NAME

Remember my name. I am the person you said I could not become. The person I wanted to be. You doubted me and never believed in my dreams – told me what I could and couldn't do. You tried to box me in, but I live outside the box.

You tried to hold me back because of your own regrets. Now I can see that the person I am, is the person you desired to be. You see, I am the one following my dreams - which you can't stand - because you always wanted to do the same but did not have the heart to follow through.

Your constant criticism of what I am doing only keeps me motivated. It actually keeps me going - because I know I'm going to be somebody. Your laughter at my stumbles only makes me work harder. What you don't know is that I can never fail; each time I fall is a lesson learned, which keeps me winning.

Keep doubting me – and watch as I keep breaking through barriers to reach my goals. Some people only get one shining moment. However, I am preparing for many shining moments.

Keep trying to hold me back with your negative thoughts. While you're trying to trip me up, I'm thinking, "It's alright, I'm going to make it anyway, with or without your support." I know where I'm going in my life because I, with the help of God, am directing my path. Can you say the same?

Go ahead and treat me differently - call me an outcast - I can take it. It used to bother me when you called me a rebel or a renegade. However, I now realize that is the only thing that you have been right about. I am a renegade - rebelling from your tired ways - just as the Saints and Prophets have throughout history. Like them, you will *remember my name.*

10

HUNTING OF GOOD WILL

He is intelligent and full of potential. However, he is also lazy, carefree about life and has many qualms. His name is Will – and a movie was made about him.

Many see his endless potential and question why he is an under-achiever. He could hold the world in his hands - but doesn't grab ahold of it. Will is smart in every aspect; he has book smarts, common sense, street smarts and is very worldly. Others cannot understand how things come so easily to Will - yet it seems that he's choosing to make his life harder than it has to be.

What no one sees is that Will is scared. Will is afraid of leaving his friends and family behind. Will is paralyzed by a fear of the unknown and the uncertainty that life holds. He doesn't even want to try because he's secretly afraid that he will fail. Carefree is he - because life scares the hell out of him.

There are few people that understand Will. Not many can see what he sees. They tell him that he owes it to himself to live up to the potential, find his greatness and be the person he was born to be. In the movie, his friend, an average Joe, tells him that he does not just owe it to himself to be someone special, but also to his friends.

Most of you realized long ago, way before I did, that I am Will. You saw my potential before I even knew what my potential was. What you can't see is that I'm afraid to fail - because I would be letting you all down. Yet, I'm also afraid to succeed – because it means leaving family and friends behind. The world is so cold and lonely enough already. Or is it just that I don't believe in myself the way that you all believe in me?

A wise man once told me to follow my heart and let my fears go. I think I am finally ready to take that advice. Like everyone, I am hunting for Good Will. It's time to make an effort, leave my fears behind and live up to my potential. I'm grateful for *Good Will Hunting*, because I now know that he - is me.

11

POWERLESS

Censor my words. Tell me how to think, how to act and what to say. Exploit my culture and image. Tell me what to wear and how to style my hair. Treat me unfairly because of my wealth or lack thereof. Make me dislike who I am. Make me lighter or darker than I seem. Make me ignore my ancestry. Tell me that I am too skinny or too fat. Show me that straight hair is beautiful and that anything different isn't beautiful at all. Make me feel *powerless*.

However, I am going to say what I want. Dress how I feel. I am beautiful just the way I am. Whether I weigh too much or too little for you, or my skin is too light, white or dark for you, I fit in because I am not trying to fit in. I have nothing to prove to you. I am a rebel because I choose not to follow your rules – instead I make my own rules. I do not need to follow the path that you made for me. In doing so I would be *powerless*.

Instead I'll carve out my own path and learn from my own mistakes. I will never forget where I come from and who I am. What you do not understand is that my life is just too short to live just for you. You have no effect on me because your rules and stereotypes do not concern me at all. *You are powerless.*

12

SELL-OUT AND A NIGGER

It's sad that no matter what I accomplish in my life I will always be a nigger to you because of the color of my skin. I'm tired of being harassed when I try to get into "your" so called bars, colleges, jobs, movies, etc. All I want is to have the same opportunities that you have, but you consistently push me down. Why? Because I am of a darker complexion than you.

On the other hand, even some of my own race will consider me a sell-out for striving to make a difference and take advantage of the opportunities that are before me. My brother, don't you see that in bettering myself, I am bettering us - not as a single race but as the whole human race? However, you do not see that - because all you see is that I am trying to be better than you - by going to school, having a career and not hanging out in the streets.

Well, my friends, how much do I have to prove to earn something in your eyes? Whether you think that I haven't struggled enough - or that I don't know what it feels like to be treated as an outcast without a voice in this world – I'm certain that you have never experienced life's struggles from my point of view. Have you been excluded by other races and even some of your own people, despite the fact that you're a respectable, hardworking, goal-driven human being? Have you consistently been discriminated against, felt like you did not have a voice, and we're being prejudged before people even got to know you? It's frustrating and defeating to work as hard as I have, just to get knocked down on both fronts. But I will not give up.

I see what you try to deny. That is, that both of you fear me - I am your worst nightmare. I am the *Dream* that Dr. King envisioned. I am diverse in my taste, my intellect, influences and activities. Some of you treat me as a nigger because you're scared to compete with me - so you try to disqualify me before the competing even begins. However, I do not want to compete against you. I just want to be afforded the same opportunities. And some of you call me a sell out because you are afraid of trying, of succeeding, of getting out of your comfort zone. So, call me whatever you want - but I am neither the nigger, nor the sell-out. In the meantime, I'm going to continue to take advantage of the opportunities before me – until you all can get it together and get on the bus.

13

REGRETS

I regret hurting my loved ones. I regret not taking advantage of many of the opportunities that have come my way. I regret giving all of my heart - only to have it broken. Also, I regret the hearts that I have broken. I regret not saying I love you more often. I regret all the shame I caused you and all the lies that I have told you. I regret the things that I have stolen. I regret not trying my hardest and giving my all. I regret not living up to my potential and expectations. I regret expecting too much of you. I regret the pressure I put on you. I regret my short, bad temper. I regret giving up so easily. I regret not giving up at all. I regret wanting something so badly that I felt crushed after falling short of reaching it. I regret my tendency to procrastinate. I regret my negative experiences and the negative experiences that I have caused others.

However, I can truly say that I do not regret who I am. So in reality, I do not have any REGRETS - because all these things have helped shape me to become the person I am.

14
CHANGE IN ME

It's not about where I've been, it's about where I'm going. Do not look at the person I was, but instead see me for the person I am now. You're not the same person you were yesterday either. Sometimes we change for the better – sometimes for the worse. Please notice the changes that I have made. If they have made me better, please be proud of me; if they have made me worse, then please do me the favor of praying for me - instead of talking about me and leaving me be.

The change in me occurs from the mistakes I've made - the lessons I have or have not learned. I may stumble and fall - or I may succeed and accomplish my goals - but I do not fault anyone for my mistakes. It's the failing and succeeding that brings growth, which leads to the greatest change in me.

I ask you to not only look at where I've been and remember the person I once was – but also to see where I'm going and the person I have now become. Only then, will you understand the change in me.

15
COURSE THREE

Soups & Salads/Brain Food

"Motivation is like food for the brain. You cannot get enough in one sitting. It needs continual and regular top ups." Peter Davies

16
FEAR

Fear comes from the unknown or a lack of understanding. It can be crippling - and has the potential to make each of us a prisoner. When fear makes us doubt ourselves, it becomes our worst enemy. Uncontrolled fear can even lead to stress, illness and a premature death.

In the animal kingdom, rabbits are faster than lions – yet, more times than not, a lion will catch its prey (the rabbit). The lion's secret weapon is its loud roar, which can be heard as far as three miles away. When the rabbit is just about to escape the hunt, the lion unleashes this loud roar which strikes fear into the heart of the rabbit, causing it to immediately become frozen in its tracks. As a result, the lion now has its meal.

Similarly, people will often let fear stop them from trying anything new or challenging. The news is constantly showing us negative things that are happening in the world, which cause us, like the rabbit, to freeze up and not live our lives freely. Government abuses make us suspicious, terror alerts have us afraid to travel, and reports of shark attacks make us fear going into the ocean. However, they will not tell you that you have a better chance of winning the lottery or being struck by lightning than being attacked by a shark.

While some things in life are inevitable, like falling and getting hurt, sickness, broken hearts and even death - fearing these things will only cause us to fall harder, hurt more and love less. Successful people take that fear and redirect it in ways that lift them up. They are more afraid of not living – than failing. They do not fear falling out of the sky – but instead learn how to fly. Your mind can be your best friend or your worst enemy. Face your fears and you will find that fear is nothing but an illusion.

17
INSANE

Insane is what you call me because of my spirituality. Materialistic things do not move me. *Insane* is what you call me because I am being me. Just because I'm different and don't follow the crowd, I am an outcast. Fine, then that is what I will be - but don't blame me because I rage against the machine. I ruffle feathers, talk to spirits, and sense the kind of person someone is by the energy or aura they gave off. Just because I see and know things that other people don't - and am not afraid to admit it - you want to institutionalize me and throw away the key.

Yes, my moods go up and down. I am a human being. Isn't that what our emotions are for? Perhaps I am happy one moment because I think my soul has won the fight with my flesh; then I'm sad because my body is once again doing something that my soul does not agree with. Maybe my moods are erratic because I see the potential of this world – then realize our current state – and it upsets me.

For years, people like me have been labeled as bi-polar, manic depressive and schizoid because we see what you care not to see. To me, true insanity would be to shut my eyes and not say a word about what's going on. You can continue to judge and label me - but you can never kill my spirit - because it is God's.

So when you call me *insane*, you are really complementing me. The great books say that the unbelievers will try to make the people that know, feel as if they are not sane. So I ask you, am I really the one that is *insane*, or is it you?

18
DISPLACED REALITY/UNCONSCIOUS GUSTING SABOTAGE

You depend on me, thinking that I am a friend. However, in reality I am your biggest foe. Your displaced reality has you thinking that you need me to make you happy. You can count on me to make a party more fun. I am there to take the pain away - or so you think. You see, when I'm around you, I make you forget your problems. Foolishly, you think when I'm not around, your problems grow bigger.

When did we meet? I cannot remember, but I will not forget *how* we met. Whether through a friend, lust, temptation or peer pressure, one thing is for sure - once that I am in your life it's hard to get me out of it.

Some athletes depend on me to get stronger or faster. Some people depend on me to relieve their pain physically, emotionally or mentally. Some depend on me to lift them up when they are down - and others want me to bring them down when they are up. One thing is the same for everyone that depends on me - I will destroy your life sooner or later.

I take the money that you need to support yourself and your family and make you spend it on me. I will make you moody. You often turn on your loved ones when they tell you to leave me. I destroy friendships and families. It pleasures me to see babies crying because you spent their food money on me. Don't you see, people kill for me! I am a *Gusting Wind of Sabotage* but you are unconscious because of me - and are blind to see.

Because of me, people become rich and others become poor. Countries fight wars using the wealth that I bring them. Companies invest in me. In return, I make their investments turn into billions.

I am both legal and illegal. I am natural and artificial. I can cure you - and I can kill you. I am a solid, a liquid and a gas. I can be taxed but most of the time I am not taxed at all. I am your *Displaced Reality of Unconscious Gusting Sabotage*. In other words - I am DRUGS.

19
MOMENT OF TRUTH (CLARITY)

In every life, we must eventually face the *moment of truth*. You can be on the top - or the bottom - the moment of truth will not discriminate. Even when your problems seem insurmountable, do not fear. You've been through struggles before and it's in those moments that you find clarity. You learn how strong you are, who your true friends are, and you can plainly see the wrong turns that you have made.

Live life treating others as you want to be treated. Remember, in the end, everyone will get what he or she deserves - just as you will get what is due to you. Don't be too quick to judge - because you don't know what someone's life has been like – or what they're going through now.

It is in the midst of the pain that you will find your strength. Problems help you get rid of unnecessary baggage, negativity and pride. You will see that this newfound clarity will justify all the suffering. Evil cannot stay on top forever -

and when you can find meaning in the pain – it ceases. This is your moment of truth.

20
COLOR BLIND

I had a so called "friend" tell me the other day that I only like "white" music and date white women. This is not the first time I've fallen prey to this type of judgment, except it's usually said that I listen to ghetto music and just date black women. I find this funny, or maybe a little sad, because I swore that when it came to music, love, happiness, pain and friendship – I would not see color.

Good music is simply good music, regardless of the genre. If a person can relate to it, then they should embrace it. As long as a couple is truly in love then nothing else matters. So why is it a problem when people become friends with those of different races, colors and gender? Why is it a problem when a person loves someone that looks different than them?

Everyone wants the same things in life - happiness, comfort and love. These feelings and emotions are color blind. So, why should it matter if a person is white, yellow, brown or green if they make you happy? That applies to all areas of life – including music, politics, friendship and love.

People need to diversify themselves and stop letting color or race block them from enjoying the best things that life has to offer. It is time for people to open their minds, become color blind and unite.

21
IF!

If – it is one of the smallest words, yet holds so much power for mankind. People love the word *if* and use it often, but what does it really mean? Nothing. *If* is simply imaginary.

We say, "If I had a million dollars," "if I was worried," "if I did this," "if I did that," "if I would have known." This one little word is extremely powerful because it enables us to cope with what's really going on. It allows us to deny reality. How many times have people used the word *if* to justify something? For example, "If I stole the money, then why am I still broke?"

Many times, we use the word to express doubt about ourselves and entertain worst case scenarios, such as "what if I miss this shot" or "if I ask him/her out, they'll laugh at me." Instead, we should use the word *if* to enhance our hope and ability – by saying, "If I ask him/her out, they will respect me" and "If I make this shot," etc.

The word *if* can cause us to feel hope, pain, denial or doubt – all depending on the way that we use it. A wise friend once told me to replace the word *if* with *when* – because a positive mind allows positive things to happen. Instead of saying "if I win the lottery," one should say "when I win the lottery." Who would have thought that such a little word could be so powerful?

22
REAP WHAT YOU SOW

Positivity cannot come forth if a positive seed is not planted.

Love cannot be received if love isn't given.

Answers will not come if questions aren't asked.

If you are always serious, you will miss out on fun - and if you play all the time, who will take you seriously?

Those who are blessed give to charity.

Those who are continuously surrounded by drama and negativity, love it – otherwise they wouldn't be around it so much.

The wise spend time learning.

To be great, hard work is needed.

In order to gain respect, respect has to be given.

You get what you give.

Some say its karma - some call it the Law of Attraction.

It is simply reaping what you sow.

23
TAKE RISKS, GET OUT OF YOUR COMFORT ZONE

Everyone wants security in life, but what constitutes security? How long does it last? Is there really even such a thing?

Many people stay in jobs they dislike because it offers them financial security. They can't wait for the weekend to come so they can get a break from their jobs – yet they will let thoughts of returning to their jobs ruin their weekend. The need for comfort and security, and the fear of not having it, causes people to settle - but placing yourself in a box is not really living at all. It places limits on what you can do. Being too comfortable stunts our growth – and can cause us to miss out on many of life's greatest pleasures.

Living is much more enjoyable when you're doing something that you love. In fact, that is the difference between simply having a job and having a career. Getting out of one's comfort zone and taking risks allows people to use their natural instincts, hone their survival skills and know their limits. Being brave enough to face your fears will not only enable you to excel in life but also to discover who you truly are.

Don't be afraid to fly. Many of us go along simply doing what society expects of us. Unfortunately this makes us just dreamers - not people who are following their dreams. If you want to become a singer, basketball player, doctor, lawyer, or entrepreneur - do it, don't think about it. Don't worry about your money situation, or what people will think or say. Just take the risk and you will find that your survival instincts will come alive to guide you. At first, money may be tight - but you will get by fine and the money will come. The main thing is to remember that money does not bring true happiness. It helps us in many ways, but it means nothing if you're not being true to yourself.

Another reason people don't take risks is because they care too much about what someone else may think. This is just an excuse for not trying. News for you, the people that love you are going to love you regardless of what you do. The people who truly love you only want you to be happy. The fact of the matter is that we let money, and what others think of us, control our lives to the point that our lives are not ours anymore.

"It's a Bitter Sweet Symphony this life,
Trying to make ends meet,
You're a Slave to MONEY then you die,"

(Lyrics from *Bitter Sweet Symphony* / The Verve)

Stop complaining that you're stuck in a dead-end job and do something about it. Be about it, dream about it, do it and live it. Stop saying, "I will try" - either do it or don't. Stop saying *"if"* and start saying *"when."* Realize that there are going to be many hard times and sacrifices, but that is what life is made of. If you are going to have to go through hard times (and we all inevitably do) then you might as well do it for something you love.

We all have the choice to lead or follow, be the leader. Remember that people in worse positions than you took the initiative to become who they wanted to be – and succeeded. The winners are those that desire to fly so badly that they don't fear falling out of the sky. The only true failure is not giving it a shot. No matter what comes your way, know that you are going to be okay – because you are giving your all - and life rewards that.

24
RELAXATION

People have become so preoccupied with their jobs and other responsibilities that they've forgotten to make time for relaxation. Some people have not de-stressed in so long that they've forgotten how. A constant lack of relaxation can be harmful and lead to many physical and mental illnesses.

There are plenty of ways to relax, so it's important to find one that works for you. Try getting a professional massage, or taking a nice, long bath or shower. Go sit in a quiet place - at the beach, park, field, or anywhere that it is just you and nature. Just be alone and free your mind from thoughts of the world and your problems. This is a form of meditation.

Relaxation helps to return us to our natural state; a mental, physical, emotional, and spiritual state where stress and worry do not reside. Close your eyes, take a deep breath and free your mind of any worrisome thoughts. Simply be at peace - and feel what you haven't felt in a very long time. That feeling, my friend, is relaxation.

25
FRIENDS

The word *friend* gets thrown around just as much as the word *love*. However, many people do not know how to be a true friend - or even what a true friend is. Friendship is not defined by the length of time two people have known each other. Also, just because you and another person do everything together does not necessarily mean you are friends.

Friends can go days, weeks, months and even years without seeing or speaking to one another but when they do reconnect, it's as if nothing has changed, they're as comfortable with each other as ever. A true friend tells you what you *need* to hear - not what you would like to hear. And when you're on the receiving end of that truth, you won't hold it against your friend because you know that they're just looking out for your best interest.

Friends treat each other with respect and take each other's feelings into consideration at all times. They treat each other like they would want to be treated. Most of all, friends are there when you need them. They take the time to help you when you have a problem. They don't just come around when it's convenient - or only when it is time to have some fun. If your "friends" only call you to go out to have fun but aren't there when times get rough, then it's time to re-evaluate who your true friends are.

26
FUN

What is fun to you?

Will your fun lead to your destruction?

Do you have to disregard your morals for fun?

Is that even truly fun?

Is a short time of pleasure and fun worth a lifetime time of

remorse and regrets?

Does your fun usually end in some kind of drama?

Is this fun at the end?

27
TIME

The sun doesn't wait for us; time stands still for no one. Is time our friend or our foe? It really all depends how you use it, and that is entirely up to you.

Time can heal a broken heart - but make yesterday a distant memory. Time flies when you're having fun - but it doesn't seem to move at all when you're in pain or are waiting for something. Time allows us to come of age, embark on life's journey into death - and then starts life all over again as the cycle repeats itself. The future becomes the present and the present moves into the past. Time is continuous - so hold onto each of life's moments - and enjoy the ride.

28
BELIEVE

I've learned that the only time that I doubt myself is when I let others lead me to it. In truth, you have to believe in yourself before anyone else will, and even then, one should not care if anyone else does or not. Believe in God - and yourself - and anything can be accomplished.

It's funny how we are the only species that need to see a sign, or receive other's approval, in order to feel justified to move forward. Other species simply work off of instincts and faith (belief in the unseen). We doubt that we can achieve our goals and put things off thinking we're going to see the next day – but time isn't promised. The next second is unseen.

It is said that having the faith of a mustard seed can move mountains. Anything is possible through the Creator of all, which strengthens me. No matter the religion, with God we can do any and all things. So when we doubt ourselves, we doubt God. Have faith and believe.

Be that mustard seed that moves mountains. Let the unbelievers keep doubting and don't be concerned with their thoughts. Unbelievers do not know the abilities of God. They do not believe in themselves, this is why they can't believe that anyone else can achieve the "impossible."

29
WHATEVER YOU DO, DON'T GIVE UP

Life has its ups and downs. When life gets hard it's important to stay positive. The troubled times of life will cause confusion. This is when you must have faith and let that faith guide you. When you're on a short rope, don't let go - keep holding on tight because everything will be alright. Let life's hardships make you more determined. With determination comes motivation. Then comes dedication. Be determined, motivated and dedicated to getting over the hardships. When problems come near, dig deep and remember that no matter what, you must not give up.

30
SUCCESS

What is success and how do we obtain it? Many people attribute success to how much money they have, what kind of car they drive or the size of their home. However, should material items really define success?

True success is gained not only from the achievement of our goals but also from the happiness and satisfaction derived from pursuing those goals. To become successful, one has to have - and keep - a plan on how they will obtain success. Keep improving and increasing your work ethic. Whether you want to become an athlete, musician, speaker, entrepreneur, model, etc., train to become the best at what you do. Give it your all. Work as hard, or harder, as the top professionals in that field.

Know that you will experience some failure along the way - but it's important to remember that failure is a necessary step on the road to success. You've heard it before; *it's not how many times you fall that matters; what matters is how many times you stand back up.* When you keep reaching for your goals - then look back to see how far you've come since falling – it is the failures that allow you to achieve a sense of satisfaction, no matter where you are on your journey.

Sometimes, in order to reach success, one has to be a little selfish. Some may criticize you for the necessary choices you must make in order to obtain your goals – but remember it's easier for people to criticize than it is for someone to create. Cast doubt, fear, and intimidation out of your mind, body and soul. Do not let pressures of other's get you down.

When you do become successful, do not boast about your success but instead let your actions speak for themselves. Strive to make a positive difference in the world and spend your free time learning new things and continuing to be constructive. Success does come with a price – it may mean spending less time on personal enjoyment – and some people may become jealous of your success, affecting your relationships in unforeseen ways. However, if your priorities and values are in order, the success you achieve will be well worth it - and the people that truly matter will be able to share in that success with you.

31
PURITY

What do air, unpolluted water, children and animals have in common? They are all innocent and pure in nature. A baby is born into the world free of sin. You see, nature exhibits itself with purity - until mankind interferes.

Children are pure in their thoughts, interactions, moods and experiences. They do not entertain the notions of race, discrimination or prejudice. A child comes into the world without self-doubt and is excited to try something new and interesting. Children are moved by their feelings – they eat, use the restroom and sleep when they need to. A child loves everyone.

Although we may think we're protecting them, adults end up taking away the purity of children. We teach them to doubt themselves because we are afraid to try things. We make them eat, sleep and live on our schedules because we already have a set routine. We set the example of seeing race because we cannot look past someone's skin color. Children are not ashamed of who they are. It's funny how children can play with each other no matter how another child looks. Children can get mad at each other - and five minutes later they're playing together again. Yet adults hold grudges over the pettiest things and do not forgive easily.

Perhaps we have it backwards - children should not be learning from us - we should be learning from them. We would take on new challenges with excitement, eat and sleep when we needed to, love everyone and forgive easily. Racism wouldn't exist.

I don't know about you - but I want to be as pure as the water that flows from the springs. I want to go back to my childhood - to a time when everything was innocent and peaceful.

32
FREEDOM

People all over the world search for freedom - and some also fight for it. Many are waiting for a government, or some power, to give them freedom. However until the people realize that freedom cannot be given to them, they will never be free. Freedom comes from within a person. To truly be free we must first free our minds. We must all look deep inside of ourselves and release ourselves from the physical, mental, spiritual, financial, and emotional prisons that we subject ourselves to daily. We must be opened-minded, forgiving, peaceful, loving, and faithful. Letting the government, or one who is in power, determine our freedom of speech, expression, and rights is not freedom at all. True freedom lies within you – and you alone.

33
IN CASE YOU FORGET

As you complain that you have to get out of bed today because you are sick, there's a little girl out there that is living with cancer, not complaining and grateful that she can get out of bed. As you are at work, hating the job that you have, remember that there is someone that is wishing they had your job.

As you complain about your limited rights and lack of freedom, think about others that do not have rights and have never known freedom. Better yet, think about the people from all races, genders, creeds, and religions that fought, and sometimes died, for the rights and freedom that you have.

As you complain about your speech, hearing and sight; Imagine how it would be if you were a person that couldn't talk, hear or see. Would that make you appreciate what you have more?

In case you forget that you are blessed, take a closer look around you. You will see that you really don't have it bad at all.

34
LIFE IS AMAZING

Time flies by so easily – except for when the hard times come. Funny, we can never make up our minds, do we want time to slow down or do we want it to move faster? They say that *life is crazy*, but perhaps we are the crazy ones.

What is the meaning of life? Life has so many meanings. It takes pain for us to know joy. It takes living to know death - and it takes death to show us that we take life for granted. We wait forever to find true love, but then it only takes a minute to actually fall in love. In the winter it is cold and we cannot wait for summer's heat to warm us. When summer's heat arrives, we can't wait for a cool winter's breeze to offer us relief. Rain falls, flowers grow, day is gone and night has come. Life is so complete. Life goes full circle.

We say life is confusing, but I say we are the ones that are confused. It takes seeing our trash become someone else's treasure for us to realize that it wasn't trash at all. Even funnier is that you cannot have success without knowing failure. To see how strong we are, and to get stronger, we must be tested. To be a leader, you must first be a follower. Children want to grow up fast to be adults; adults want to become kids again.

Life is many things - but crazy is not one of them. Life is wonderful. Life is amazing. We are the crazy ones. Life teaches us lessons by the minute.

35
COURSE FOUR

Entrée / Soul Food

"Love is our deepest longing. Just as the body needs food, the soul needs love – it is nourishment, spiritual nourishment. Without food, air and water the body will deteriorate; without love the soul starts shrinking." - Osho

36
LOVE

So many have written about love, yet it seems that we don't truly understand this complicated emotion. We know that there are different kinds of love - love for a family member, love for a friend, and even love for an object, activity or pastime. And, of course, there is the love one has for a romantic companion, which we refer to as "being in love."

There are also different types of love. Conditional love is when one loves something or someone only when the conditions (time, health, mood, etc.) are right or "perfect." For example, some people love their companions until other difficult factors come into play, such as health problems, mental problems, drug habits, or betrayal.

The opposite of conditional love is "unconditional love" – which involves a devoted dedication, no matter what happens. This is what marriage vows are built upon; "through sickness or health, richer or poorer..." Perhaps the world would become a better place if we could all find more unconditional love in our hearts.

One thing the human species needs to understand is that love affects each of us differently. People are constantly trying to define love by using words like happiness, trust, communication and loyalty. However, those things do not define love at all. When you love something or someone, it doesn't mean that you're always happy. A couple can lose their trust or communication - but that doesn't mean there isn't any love there. Parents may not always trust, communicate well, or be happy with their children - but they love them still.

One thing is for sure, just when we think we have love all figured out, it will throw us a curve-ball. It cannot easily be defined. We all love differently, and therefore it has different lessons for each of us.

37
A GREAT COMPANION

Irreplaceable is *she* - I met her at 19 years of age - a sophomore in college. The first time I saw her, I knew she was special but I had no idea how she would impact my life. She was a five-foot-three, French-vanilla complexioned beauty - and she was my first true love. She showed me many things in life, including what a true *lady* was about. We made the journey from adolescence to adulthood together. We held each other down through the pain and struggle, yet we also enjoyed many moments of pleasure and happiness together. We even tattooed each other's names on our bodies. After three-and-a-half years together, it was time to call it quits. However, we will be friends forever - and *she will remain Irreplaceable.*

She was ebony-complexioned, tall, beautiful and five years my junior. Yet she carried herself years beyond her age. A basketball star, with the brains of a doctor and the innocence of a baby, she was extremely humble. I was her first love -

and her first true relationship. Being older, one would think that I would have been the *teacher*, but it was she who taught me what a true relationship should be. She pushed me beyond, to levels that I didn't believe I could reach. Although our time together was short, *she is Unforgettable*.

I've known her since the eighth grade but would have never imagined that ten years later we would be dating. *She* is a small statured, fiery redhead with a heart as big as the ocean. Although we never put a label on *us*, for four years she took care of me. Let me just say that it was me that did not want to commit. Still she stayed around, even though I was not giving her all my attention. Patiently, she waited for me to change my ways even though I hurt her constantly. Like *Ms. Irreplaceable* and *Ms. Unforgettable*, she believed in me even when I didn't believe in myself. It crushed me when I crushed her heart. However, she stayed strong even until the day she stopped waiting on me to give her my attention. As I look back and see what I put her through, I realize how she handled it all with such grace. This is why *she is Unbelievable* to me.

She is a quiet, little redhead (or should I say orange) that I met in the sixth grade and have remained friends with over the years. Chemistry is something we have never lacked. However, these last five years have become a redundant game that I've grown tired of playing. Every year around August we reconnect - usually after one of us have ended a relationship. We engage in deep conversation and then hook up, which is always great. This lasts for a couple of weeks until we reach that threshold of being in a relationship. All of a sudden, communication breaks down and we drift apart for months. However, when one calls - the other comes running. Thus leading me to admit, *she is Irresistible*.

She has been one of my best friends since the first day we arrived on campus together – when I saw the same thing in her eyes that she saw in mine. Acting on it was another story. Although we came close many times, a bond like ours is rare and need not be broken. Perhaps, we feel this desire for each other because we are so much alike. Perhaps, we do not take the risk because we are both untamable. Maybe, the real risk would be taming ourselves for one another. Until we figure this "thing" out, we will keep pretending that the white elephant isn't in the room. However, everyone else sees what we clearly avoid. This is why *she is so Undeniable*.

She is the mother of my son, and when I met her I could see the pain in her eyes. Help is all I wanted to do, even when others told me to stay away. Help is what I gave; yet hurt is all she tries to give in return. I understand where she has been, so her efforts can never hurt me. See, *she has been hurt* and left by everyone that has been close to her - so pain is all she knows - so pain is what she gives. However, love

81

and help is what I will continue to give because *she is Understandable.*

While our history will never be erased and our memories will never fade - I fall away from a past that follows me - in hopes that I will find my future life-long partner. *She* will be a piece of Ms. Irresistible, Ms. Unforgettable, Ms. Irreplaceable, Ms. Unbelievable and Ms. Undeniable. Whoever this special lady is/will be, *she is Unimaginable* to me as of now. Perhaps, she may always be Unimaginable - even when I find her and settle down.

38
DEEP LOVE

Alone is no way to live - so I am out to find that someone who can bring me high. Higher than the stars in the sky. Someone that is my best friend – just like June Carter was to Johnny Cash. Someone to lift me up when I am low. Someone to be there for me in every need and every way. Yes, I have been in love before, but what I am searching for is a *Deep Love*.

Hey love, although I have yet to find you, my friends and I talk about you all the time. I am not a worthy man. I come with flaws, faults and a record that is far from clean. However, what is a king without a queen?

When I do find you, you shall be the perfect woman – or at least the perfect lady for me. Even your faults will make you more perfect in my eyes. I want to live that line from *Jerry McGuire*, and know that "you complete me."

They say behind every great man is a great woman. Hell, even rodents find *Deep Love*, just ask Mickey and Minnie. I'm looking to be like Ossie Davis and Ruby Dee. I don't know whether I'm coming or going - and I need someone who understands. Come set me free, because for you I will wait until Kingdom come. Oh *Deep Love,* could it be that you are waiting for me too? If so, please just wait for me. This feeling is hard to find but alone is no way to live - we can love one another.

39
IN THE AIRPORT

I arrive with suitcase in hand, tired from being up all night spending my last hours in town with friends. In line, I stand impatiently waiting to check in. I overhear a family next to me talking, as if they're reading my mind. "The check-in lady is so rude," says the girl in the family. *My thoughts exactly*, I say to myself.

When I'm finally checked in, I still have an hour before boarding. At least I have one of my best friends with me, waiting for a flight of his own. As we pass the time reflecting on the past, I notice lovers and loved ones saying their goodbyes. Before long, it's our time to say our farewells as we travel to our respective checkpoints. I give my boy a hug and a pound before we set off on our travels. While I'm sad to now be alone, I am excited to be on this journey. I watch families of all ages, business men and women, college students and people of all races traveling in harmony.

As I board the plane and find my seat I take notice of the other passengers - some are nervous, some are excited and others look peaceful. As for me, I am as sleepy as one can be. I waste no time going to sleep. When I awake, I have just arrived at another airport.

We all get off the plane. For some this is their final destination. For others, like myself, this is just the halfway point. I walk hastily as I try to make it to my terminal. "F!" is what I say, while I wonder, "Why is this terminal so far away?" With just fifteen minutes between flights, how will I get there in time?

Somehow, I make it with time to spare. A frantic lady comes up to TSA stating that her son has run off. We all search for about two minutes before the little boy is found. As I now stand waiting to board my connecting flight, I hear the little boy crying because his mom is fussing at him for scaring her half to death. When I glance around to make sure everything is alright - time stands still. It stands still because a gorgeous lady walks by, and at that moment, I know that she is the ONE. In amazement (most certainly with my mouth wide open), I look towards my right where a man looks at me with a nod of the head and whispers, "Yes, she is beautiful."

Still in shock, I now board the plane and whom do I see? *Beauty* is her name. She waits to get into her seat, and as I walk past, we stare at each other - you know, the "I like what

I see" stare. I take my seat without saying anything. I sit between two college students. We have a nice conversation but all I'm thinking about is getting to the airport. Will I see *Beauty* in the airport?

At last, we land, but as I wait for others to get their carry-ons – I notice that she has already gotten off the plane. *Oh well, you win some, and you learn some* is my motto.

The five-hour journey, mixed with my lack of sleep, is really kicking in. I almost forgot that I have to go to baggage claim to wait for my other bag. *Oh my, there she goes.* How is she the only passenger still waiting for her luggage? She walks up to me, asks me a question, and places her earphones in my ears so that I can listen to a song I've never heard before. All of her attention is on me, as mine is on her. Information is shared as our bags come around. My friend comes over to tell me that my ride is waiting outside. *Beauty* and I glance at each other to say goodbye. As I walk out of the door and into the car, I think, "Damn, what a fool I am!" I got her information, but didn't get the most important part - her name and phone number.

I sit daily waiting for the moment I will see her again. She haunts my thoughts and my dreams - as I reflect on that moment we had in the airport.

40
HIDE AND SEEK

I sit on the beach, looking up at the moon and the stars
shining.

The calm and the light from outer space resemble the easy
glow you give off.

It's getting cold now. I'm in need of a warm touch.

I begin to think about you.

We are playing a game of hide and seek, except this game has
been going on since birth.

When I'm not looking, that's when you tag me and say
"You're it," knowing I'm not ready.

But when I am ready, you are nowhere to be found.

That's alright, you can run but I'm right behind you.

And you can hide, but I will find you.

How can you be so close, but so far away - like you're on the
other side of the world?

You are like an oasis and I'm in a desert.

You said you'll be my Wonder wall and you'll catch my fall.

You sting.

Like a child you forget, but unlike you I remember

everything.

Tired of this long game.

But we'll both remain the same.

Hide and seek, you are to blame.

41
MY LOVE

Since I first laid eyes on you, I knew I wanted you in my life forever. When I first touched you, I felt a connection that was not expected. For a moment I felt as if I was the *chosen one*. However, you just like to play games – games that are crushing my heart and confusing my brain. So I try to forget you and keep my distance. Just when I think I am finished and over you, you come back - telling me that you love me. You call me when I'm asleep just to talk. You tell me what to read, listen to and watch so I can connect more with you. I am continuously bettering myself, improving my weaknesses and strengths for you.

However, like everything that's beautiful, you have others sprung off of you. When you give them your time and show them your true self - they leave you, disrespect you, and stop working hard for your love. You told them how you felt for them, asked them if they were ready for all that you can offer them, but they never stepped up and replied to you.

So here I am, the one that has always been there - always working hard - always there when you needed me. So it is my time to ask you, what are your true feelings and thoughts of me. Keep in mind, I ask you this after you tell me we look great together and we need to spend more time together. Yet, you never answered my question, just like those people that never responded to you. Does that make you a hypocrite? You hold a grudge because they didn't answer you – but instead walked away. Would you blame me if I held a grudge against you?

Beautiful you are, I guess you are in season and too busy for me. I will sit here just watching you. I will wait for you, working on my skills until you say *I am the one*. And even after you tell me *I am the one*, I will still be the hardest working man you will ever know. My warning to you, hurry up because time is against us, or at least me. I am getting older - but no matter what, you will always be my love.

42
DEEPER LOVE

I am searching for you every moment, whether I realize it or not. I stumble every now and then - and sometimes I fall - but you are always there to help me up. When I lose my way, you always point me in the right direction.

I have died more times than I remember, but each time I am reborn again through your mercy. My breathing does not happen by itself. Alone is no way to live. That is why you are always right beside me, even when I turn my back on you. I guess there is a *Deeper Love* that we will never understand.

My church does not happen in buildings, it happens outside, in discussions near the oceans and seas. No need to question your existence, just look at the leaves that fall from the trees. Cures are found for diseases. You make pain into pleasure and turn my weaknesses into strengths. With you, there is never a negative experience because something is learned from everything. You made us all different and diverse, so that we can learn from each other and learn to love. I guess it all brings us closer to you. Now I understand that you are giving a *Deeper Love*.

43
DOES ANYONE FEEL WHAT I FEEL?

Child of God basking in the spirit. Strong and faithful have I been. So why am I going through so much all at one time? Does anyone else feel what I'm feeling? Can they see what I'm seeing? The ones I talk with tell me to stay strong, as if that's even a choice. Well I suppose it is. I can either get my butt whipped by life standing up - or I can be a coward and get beat lying down.

I find myself reading the scriptures and praying constantly. So why am I cursing at God, drunk off of Grey Goose and cranberry juice? I question, why do the little, innocent children suffer? God have you forsaken them? Why are so many people homeless? Why are the faithful going through so much?

Then it dawns on me. I prayed for all of this. In my prayers I asked to be stronger. How else does one become stronger other than being tested? Then an inner voice says to me, *"You almost have it."* I say, *"What else is there to figure out?*

I'm getting my butt kicked by life to become a stronger, wiser person." But just then, Justin Timberlake's song "Losing My Way" comes on – and I instantly see the bigger picture.

This is not just about me - just like the trials and tribulations of the men and women in the scriptures was not just about them. People go through tough times every day, some fight through them and others give up. I can never give up because I not only have to become stronger for myself – but also for all the others that look to me as an example. I must use my life to serve as an inspiration to help them get through their tough times. Then the inner voice returns, saying, *"Now you have it; although you cannot see them, many see you and many feel you."*

Then I said, *"God please forgive me for losing my way and thank you for not giving up on me."*

44
MERCY

I have made many mistakes. I have been on top. However, it seems that I have been on the bottom more times than not. I get knocked down - but each time His mercy lifts me back up. I seek to walk the path of the righteous.

Every time I leave the sinful life, it tries to pull me back in. Seems like every time I am starving for His time, someone is hungry for mine. His presence is what I feel constantly. His blessings are shown everywhere. Even when there seems to be no way out of my present problems and troubles - He provides a way out. Faith is what I have. There is no need to ask why I am so positive. If you didn't take your blessings for granted then you would understand. So to Him, I say, *Thank you for your mercy.*

45
COURSE FIVE

Side Dishes / World Cuisine

"Don't gain the world and lose your soul, wisdom is better than silver or gold…" - Bob Marley

46
A DREAM DEFERRED/CHANGE NOT YET COME

Today, we as a great nation celebrate. We celebrate the life of Dr. Martin Luther King Jr., as well as celebrate Barack Obama becoming the United States first African-American president. This nation, great and proud, has come a long way from the struggles and differences of yesteryear.

Yet, forgive me for not celebrating loudly with you all. Forgive me for the sadness that is on my face. However, I will not ask for forgiveness for the tears that I cry. My tears are of pain - and great joy.

My tears of joy are for the fight of our ancestors that have made it possible for history to be made today. Their pain - the marches and the beatings - were not in vain. Dr. King, along with other civil rights leaders, paved the way for this day to come.

My fellow Americans, forgive me for being the bearer of bad news in these joyous times. Although our journey has yielded some victories - the journey is far from over. We will only reach the end of the road, which we call the *Promised Land*, by lovingly joining together.

Dr. King did not just speak of equal rights for blacks. He spoke about equality among all minorities, which includes race, gender, sexual orientation, religious affiliation and social class. Dr. King also stood for peace, both abroad and at home.

However, in order for us to truly love one another and bring positive change into this world, we must first learn to love ourselves. We must become the change we want to see. President Obama is the face of change, but he cannot change the world by himself. We must all step up and make change - even when others are afraid. Men must actively become fathers to their children. Women must honor and guard their self-respect.

The dream will become a reality but we must first stand up against injustice. While we are all created equal, we are still not all treated as equals. Poverty, segregation and discrimination still exist - they are just more hidden now. The best education goes to those in higher economic classes and better neighborhoods. Programs in the lower economic communities are the first to get cut. Giving the rich more educational opportunities will not better this great nation - or the world. The goal should be for all people to live a peaceful life - so that peace will travel far and wide.

We have not yet overcome but we will overcome soon. We will not be free until all are free from oppression. Yes, change is happening - and change is coming. Keep dreaming. The *Promised Land* is at hand. So let me cry my tears of joy and pain for the greatest race, the human race. I will celebrate loudly with you all soon enough - but for bigger reasons than what is taking place now. Peace be with you.

47
COWARD

How can you sit there not saying anything as the company that you are an executive for is laying off thousands of workers? They are laying off workers to save money, while you and your friends are making well over six and seven figures. Why don't you speak up? Why don't you and your friends/colleagues take a pay cut so that other workers can stay? However, you will not - because you are a *coward*.

What is going on Mr. Follower? You are so bright. You have so many skills and talents within you. You want to stand out in the crowd - as long as a crowd is behind you. Scared to stand out on your own, scared to be different. Instead of being the trendsetter you were born to be, you are just a *coward* living in someone else's shadow.

You judge me because you are afraid to judge yourself. Your prejudiced views do not define me – they simply show your own insecurities. If you are afraid to get to know me, then don't blame your own ignorance about what you don't understand on me. Until you deal with your issues, a *coward* is all you will ever be.

You are living life on the down-low, afraid to admit who you really are. You are killing innocent people. You indulge yourself by living a double life and don't care how you hurt others. How is it fair that you are transmitting diseases to innocent females that don't know you are living a lie? You want the world to feel pity for you, but pity you do not have for the world. Stop infecting my innocent community with the diseases you carry. Until you come clean, a *coward* is all you will ever be to me.

48
(NIGGER) NIGGA NO MORE

When did it become right to use one of the most hurtful words in history in our everyday vocabulary? When did this become a term of endearment? Who decided that the words *nigger* or *nigga* are not offensive anymore?

I hear people everywhere saying it to greet one another. Whatever happened to greeting each other as *brothers*? You say it as a term of endearment when really it's a term of disrespect. Nigga and nigger sound the same to me. You think because you changed the spelling that it makes a difference? Let me tell you, you can change the spelling - but it will never change the history.

Deep down you feel me and know that I am right. If I'm not, then tell me why you get offended when it's said by someone that's white? It's a slap in the face to our ancestors that were called that daily - so why, brothers and sisters, do we call each other this daily? Tell me, shouldn't it hurt you more to be called a word of hate by your own people than by someone that doesn't know you at all?

Some of you are trying so hard to *be* niggas – but don't you see that when you get right down to it, the meaning of the word is stupid or ignorant. Don't you know that we were kings, queens and scholars? So my friends, you are not a nigger because you are black, you become one due to how you act. You are nigger/nigga because it is what someone else wants you to be. Willie Lynch would be proud if he was alive today. Some of us are so blinded that we are killing ourselves and turning our backs on each other. The lighter complexioned don't like the darker complexioned, and vice versa. Some of you are caught up in what they call "The Nigger Mind State."

To my brothers and sisters of other races, do you still want to be a nigga too? You use the term like it's cool. Let me ask you, how cool would it be if cracker, spic, chink, wetback, kyke, or grease ball, among other hateful words that offend you, were used as a term of endearment? You wouldn't like it. I guess it's cool to be a nigga/nigger until they start following, blaming, hanging, lynching and killing niggers.

I turned on the television the other day and heard the words nigger and niggas. These words weren't said on HBO, Cinemax, or Showtime - they were on a basic cable channel.

Is this what it has come to? Rightly, people are discouraged from saying faggot or retard in order not to offend homosexuals or those with a mental disability – yet, the two races that have been treated the most unjustly by this nation are still subjected to derogatory slurs. The media has "nigger/nigga" all over the TV - and the National Football League still has a team named "Redskins" - a racist slur to Native Americans. Yet not too many people have problems with this. They are still calling the *red man* a fool and the *black man* a nigger. Each day it seems that we care less and less about what's going on in our society.

I refuse to sit back and not say a word. I am going to be me - so when you address me, address me as *brother*. This, my friends, goes for people of all colors. We have to unite and take a stand - the stand to be niggers/niggas no more, no matter your race.

49
YOUTH OF A NATION/STAND UP

My feelings and opinions go without notice. I have learned to keep my thoughts and words to myself. You have made choices that you think are right for me - but they are not. You've babied me to the point where if I'm not good at something, you are willing to change the rules so I can be on even ground - instead of allowing me to work harder to become better. You think it's helping me but you're actually crippling my work ethic and making me weak. We are the *Youth of a Nation* that are not heard – yet we have a lot to say. Sooner or later you will have to listen.

I know that the world right now is dealing you a rough hand. I see that you are scared and running out of options. You are hurt and the pain is written all over your face. I know that it is hard but stand tall, things will get better.

You take away our programs and after school activities, so we join the neighborhood gangs - then you ask, "Why?" It is because our voices are not being heard. You have no time for us and you are cutting the programs that spark our intellect and interest. You blame us for where the nation is headed. However, it's not our fault when we don't have a voice or a choice in your decision-making. Or is it that you chose not to hear us? So we act out, but where does that get us? Nowhere. We become caught in a never-ending cycle. So this is my cry - my cry for the *Youth of the Nation.*

Brothers, it's natural for everyone to get scared every now and then. However, we have to stop running away. We are supposed to lead our women and children. Yet we are leaving our women and children to their own devices. It is time to man up and start respecting our women. Time to build them up - and stop tearing them down. It is time to take care of our children - and stop letting the streets raise them.

We are the *Youth of a Nation.* The youth that will one day right your wrongs. The youth that will one day be in control. The youth that will one day take care of our elders. Please stop investing in wars and foreign affairs and invest more in our music, art and after-school programs. Take time to talk with us and help us to become better people. We are the *Youth of a Nation.*

Yes, it's hard out here in the world – but now think about how hard the world is when you're alone and have no guidance. My brothers (men of all races) it is time to stand up and be leaders. It is time to take care of our responsibilities, so

112

the streets and the system will not take our responsibilities from us. It is time for us to be men.

50
THE FUTURE

Our young people need us. They are speaking out, but very few care to listen. *They* are ready to listen - but not many are taking the time to speak to them. Our youth are looking for greater understanding, as well as to be understood themselves.

Many of them are searching for love and finding it in the wrong places. However, it's not their fault. The older generation never took the time to show them what love truly is. Maybe it's because they don't even know, never learned to have self-respect, and this is simply causing our young people to follow the poor values and example of the generations before them.

What can be expected of us when we've only had minimal paths of guidance? How can someone build self-confidence when they're talked down to and never given acknowledgement for the good deeds that they do? It is human nature to forge your own path based on the approval that you get from others – unfortunately for many, approval is coming from the wrong places. Drugs, gangs, the streets, television and the wrong crowds are what most of the youth seek for approval. Who is to blame? Parents look to the teachers to help raise the youth - while the teachers say it is the parents' job. Both groups depend on society to help in guiding the youth on a positive path - however most of society seems too preoccupied with their own problems to care. The ones that do care are simply not given enough assistance to be able to help in any significant way.

The government is steadily cutting educational resources - music, art, athletic and after school programs – thus leaving our young people to spend their time in the streets, or spend too much time playing video games or watching television, instead of participating in something productive. This leads them to become disinterested in their own talents and skills because they have nothing to motivate them to improve them.

Our youth are searching for respect and love. They need to be *talked to* - not *talked down to*. They are ready to give respect - as soon as they too are respected. It is time to guide the future by supporting our young people. Parents, teachers and society as a whole, must realize that it takes a village to raise a child. By simply taking the time to listen, you will see how brilliant and talented these young people really are.

Perhaps they may even teach you a few things. One thing is for sure, they will show you how much promise the future holds.

51
JUSTICE

When it comes to man, there is no such thing as justice - it's *just us*. The justice system is just that, a system. A system is a "combination of units that function together." Policemen, lawyers and judges have each other's backs, often covering each other's steps, no matter how wrong they are. I realize that some people don't believe this, as if they are brainwashed by what society has told them, but it's time to wake up. For every injustice caught on tape, multiply that by at least one hundred. Rodney King's situation was not, and still is not, an isolated incident.

Tell me how police officers can get caught on tape beating a man over and over again and then not be charged with anything. How can police shoot a young man named Sean Bell over fifty times - stop, reload and shoot again – and then still not be found guilty of murder, manslaughter or anything else? Yet, if a civilian kills a police dog it is considered *capital murder*. When you take a moment to think about this it reinforces the idea that the justice system is only concerned with protecting their own.

I do not agree with dog fighting, however I feel that Michael Vick may have gotten a raw deal. Especially when you consider the fact that hunters will often kill their hunting dogs if they don't perform up to par, without penalty. Some would say that the difference is that one scenario involves torture and the other does not. However, it seems to me that the real difference is that the majority of the people that are dog fighting are from the "streets." While businessmen, lawyers, judges and police officers are comfortable with the idea of hunting for sport, they show little tolerance for anything that is foreign to their own lifestyles from their isolated positions of power.

It is time to treat everyone, from all walks of life, the same. One should not be penalized, or given more rights, because of their station in life. If these actions continue to happen, all trust in the legal system will be lost and the system will fall apart. There is already evidence that this is beginning to happen. It's been shown that many people who witness crimes are not stepping forward. Why? Because their trust for the police is all but gone. If the system is not for us, who is going to protect us?

52
REVOLUTION

It is time to take a stand.

Violence only begets more violence.

Innocent people are dying.

For what? Selfish ideas and agendas,

Which they think will bring them happiness.

But in the end, it only brings misery and pain.

How long will this last?

The time is now to start a Revolution.

Love is what we need.

Love conquers all.

When you love unselfishly

We all get what we need.

Love creates peace.

Love can stop wars.

Follow the Examples of

Buddha, Jesus, Moses, Muhammad,

Gandhi, Martin and Mother Teresa,

Along with others, some known, some unknown.

They all had/have the same mission,

Which is to make the world a better place.

You see, many of us think to love is to be cowardly,

Yet the only cowardly act, is to not do what is right

Because of what others think.

You can love and not get walked on.

Love doesn't mean you are a cream-puff.

So jump on the wagon

To make the world a better place.

Either way, the Revolution will start with or without you.

53
MOTHER EARTH

Earth is being raped of her resources and man is responsible. We are supposed to be the main physical protector of this wonderful place. However, we are destroying the planet by depleting her resources and filling her with negative energy. When will we stop and realize that our selfish actions are affecting much more than just ourselves?

Despite what man thinks, every creature on this earth is of importance. Our lives are inter-connected. Destroying the habitat of one organism leads to harming other life forms that depend on it for food, protection and shelter. One harmful action causes a ripple effect. At first, the ripples look small - but over time the ripples become Tsunamis which could quite possibly lead to the destruction of all creatures.

Some believe that the Earth's destruction is not their problem because they will not see it in their lifetime – they will be dead and gone long before that happens – but our actions will have a lasting effect on future generations to come. Destroying our current eco-system will leave our children and grandchildren with more health problems due to unclean air, less protection from the sunrays by depleting the ozone layer, and place stress on our world's resources furthering the devastating effects of famine. Excess pollution will make us all susceptible to sickness from eating something that was diseased because it, in turn, ate or absorbed something that was polluted.

But we can easily start rebounding the Earth - all that is needed is to make a conscious effort. The first thing we can do is increase our own positive energy. Positive energy not only enables *you* to feel empowered but it also uplifts the environment around you. Next, start recycling. With today's technology, just about anything can be recycled. Go the extra mile and pick up the litter that is around you. Keep the environment clean. Picking up excess trash not only beautifies the world but it also protects animal life. Water conservation is huge, not only are you saving water (water that millions go without) but you are saving money, as well. Support your local agriculture by shopping at farmer's markets. This cuts down on the gas and pollution that it takes to ship produce around the country. Plus the food is fresh, healthy and delicious.

Remember, there is no such thing as making a tiny difference - all effort matters. Making a few small changes can save many species' habitats, keep our own neighborhoods clean and uplifted, and create positive energy that will spread to all corners of the world.

54
MOTHER, SISTER, LOVER, BEST FRIEND

Let me apologize for what I am about to say. Trying to regain your trust has been harder than it seemed. Maybe I should start by saying that you are my sunshine, my beginning and my end. If you just could see it for yourself. You are delicate as a rose and stronger than steel. You are my mother, sister, lover and best friend.

One day you will see how beautiful you are in your own skin. No need to look in magazines to find your worth. All you will find in them are things to add to your insecurities. You see that it's your imperfections that make you perfect. If you ever get discouraged, all you have to do is take a look through history. You will find your worth in women like Cleopatra, Nefertiti, Michele Obama, Coretta Scott King, June Carter, and Oprah. The list goes on and on.

You are my backbone; without a backbone there is no support. Nations came from within you. Now all that is in you is hurt, pain and regret – and it has transformed you into something you are not. Misinformed, you believe your power is in your hips, thighs and all that's in between. You've come to feel that you must show off all of your earthly valuables in order to gain attention. Attention is what you get, but it's not the attention that you neither want nor deserve. Instead of love and respect, you are left with lust and disrespect. I know that there is more to you, but it will never matter if you do not realize what is in you. Wondering why you aren't respected? Take a look in the mirror. You have to respect yourself before I can.

It's your mind that gives you power, your heart that saves the world. Your smile warms souls, your tears cause heartache. Who else can kiss an injury and make the pain go away? Who can whisper in someone's ear and tell them that everything is alright – and then everything becomes alright? Only a mother, sister, lover and best friend.

55
WE ARE ONE

Amazing how we breathe, bleed and eat the same. We all thirst for the same basic needs in order to survive. We cried together on September 11, 2001. We've fought wars together; we were saddened by the event that took place at Virginia Tech. We also witnessed a miracle on the Hudson and had a front-row seat to history as Barack Obama was elected president.

Sadly, we allow our differences in culture, religion, and opinion to divide us from one another. Focusing on our differences leads us to overlook what is taking place in other communities. We turn our backs on the unsavory problems presented on the evening news. We see injustice and poverty - but only as long as it is not in our neighborhood.

However, when it's *our* communities that are filled with injustice, poverty and missing children, we do not understand why no one else will come to our rescue. That attitude – *if it doesn't affect me, it has nothing to do with me* – is selfish and wrong.

We are all one and the same, you see. We are the same race - *the human race*. Community injustice affects us all because when we turn our backs on these issues, we give them power. Silence and lack of action allow these problems to plague our communities, our country and the world. We are one, so we should fight to stop issues such as racism, sexism, poverty and lack of quality education – because like an untreated cancer, if you don't stop it, it will spread.

We tend to allow our differences to keep us from helping one another. We forget that we are more similar than we are different. We should learn from our diversity as human beings and not wait for tragic and historic events to happen in order for us to come together as a people. We are one nation, one world, one race and one movement. We are one.

56
COURSE SIX

Dessert / Sweet Nothings and Sour Patches

"There are two ways to live your life. One is as though nothing is a miracle. The other is as though everything is a miracle." – Albert Einstein

57
DIALOGUE BETWEEN THE PESSIMIST AND THE OPTIMIST

The Pessimist says:

The sun doesn't really like you - it is not your friend. It burns

you up,

so stay inside.

Water doesn't like you either- it swallows you up and drowns

you,

so don't go in it.

Love is not true - it always breaks your heart,

so stay out of it.

People are not kind - they always try to get over on you,

so get what you can from people and move on.

Friends, there is no such a thing as a friend - people come

and go,

so who needs them?

Happiness is short lived and always followed by sadness and

misery,

so don't waste your time trying to be happy.

In Return, *the Optimist says:*

The Sun love us - it is the main source of growth,

so bask in it.

Water loves us enough to quench our thirst and cool us off

when the sun gets too hot,

so soak it up.

Love is true - it can get you through the toughest of times,

so don't run from it.

People are very diverse - we learn from one another,

so get to know as many people as you can.

Each friend is one of a kind - and will be there when you

need them,

so surround yourself with many.

Happiness can last as long as you want - sadness and misery

simply teach you how to value joy,

so be happy.

And my friend, we need pessimistic people like you, because if no one complained we would not try to better things. The fight is only over when people stop caring enough to do something about the problem.

58
PERFECT LIAR

I told you that nothing would change between us.

You believed me, although we both knew everything would change.

I told you that we would be friends forever.

You believed me, although that kiss meant that our friendship was over.

I told you that you were the only one.

You believed me, although you saw the evidence of others in my life.

I told you that I loved you and wanted to spend forever with you.

Again you believed me, although we both know that forever is not guaranteed.

Now you tell me that I am the *perfect liar*.

I will admit that I lied to you, but you also lied to yourself,

Convincing yourself that those lies were truths.

So the *perfect liar* is you.

59
THE WRITER AND THE PEN

I am **the Pen** that allows you to express your words.

*But I am **the writer** that gives you power, you write what I want you to.*

You may think that you give me power, but I give power to your words.

If my ink doesn't flow, your ideas are not recorded.

Well, I am **the paper** that gives you both power. I am the one that you write on to get your ideas across. Without me the ink could not flow.

*Finally, **the Brain** chimes in and says:*

I am the True Creator and give each of you power.

Writer, you write what I think. Your ideas are mine. I form you in the likeness of myself - from when you eat, who you love, what you wear - I control all of it.

The ***pen and paper,*** I created you to express the feelings of this writer, and writers from all over the world.

Don't you see, neither of you have power without the other -
but together you can create something beautiful.

Yet I hardly get the credit I deserve.

You see, **the Brain** is the symbolism of GOD, **the Writer** is
humanity, **the Pen** is technology and **the Paper** is nature
itself.

60
THE SHINING

"For many are called, but few are chosen." My friends, you are some of the few that have been chosen. *The Shining* is such a special, yet difficult, gift to have. However, we must embrace it and be ourselves - take off the masks and not worry about fitting into the crowd. We stand out for a purpose. We have no control over it. The more we deny this gift, the more confusion and pain we will experience.

The Shining is the term that a few people and I use to describe the gift of having a sixth sense. We all have different reasons for calling it *The Shining*. My boy Matt says it's because the gift is scary and weird at times, like the movie "The Shining." Josh calls it *the Shining* because we are always glowing, shining and standing out, no matter the setting. Me, I say it's both. I call it *the Shining* because God gave us all the gift – but only gave a chosen few the light to realize this special gift.

If you are reading this then you are some of the chosen ones - because this isn't meant to be seen by everyone. We need to understand that being who we are helps others to embrace who they truly are. We stand out for a reason. Every follower needs a leader - and not everyone can be a leader.

Use the gift as it is meant to be used. Here are just a few people that have had the gift – and you will notice that not all of them used their gift for good: Albert Einstein, Bob Marley, Jimi Hendricks, Hitler, Tupac, Nas, Kurt Cobain, Galileo, and Gandhi.

Being in tune with *the Shining*, means you will consistently be at battle with spiritual good and flesh (earthly bad). If the enemy isn't trying to tempt you, you are not where you need to be but instead doing what he wants you to do. Also, the ones that are in-tune can always recognize others with *the Shining*. Our spirits are in control of all of this. Have you ever thought or spoken about someone and a little later that person calls or comes over? That my brothers and sisters is a spiritual connection, not coincidence. There is no such thing as coincidence. So embrace who you are – and embrace the gift.

Everything happens for a reason and God does not make mistakes.

ABOUT THE AUTHOR

Vid Lamonte' Buggs Jr. is a native of Hampton, Virginia whose main goal is to spread motivation, inspiration and love. His work serves to encourage others to look past their differences and focus on uniting to make the world a better place.

He currently resides in Tampa, Florida serving his community as a youth sports coach, mentor and motivational speaker, as well as community activist. While we all face challenges in life, his philosophy is that perseverance, positivity and a heart full of love will enable us to rise above our struggles and become the instruments to spark constructive societal change.

31703884R00097

Made in the USA
San Bernardino, CA
17 March 2016